For James, Peter and Ed, but also for
Joong Suk, Jae Sik and Jin Hyung —
the ones who got left behind

ACKNOWLEDGMENTS

Durango was commissioned by the Mark Taper Forum, Center Theater Group, Los Angeles. It was written with support from the MacDowell Colony and the Juilliard School and subsequently developed at the Eugene O'Neill Theater Conference (Wendy Goldberg, Artistic Director), the Ojai Playwrights Conference (Robert Egan, Artistic Director) and the Public Theater's New Works Now Festival (Oskar Eustis, Artistic Director).

A NOTE ABOUT PUNCTUATION

A smarter playwright than me invented the use of "/" to denote where a character begins an interruption or an overlap.

Dashes do not indicate overlap. They indicate when one word or line is *immediately* followed by the next. Please make sure the word before the dash is actually spoken.

Ellipses do not indicate overlap, but they are not exactly a pause or break. They indicate a word or thought is sustained through to the next word — left hanging, so to speak.

Words in brackets are thought and meant but not actually spoken. For example: "It's a good thing you're not ... [gay]" means that the character thinks and intends the word — and the other character understands it — but the word is left unsaid.

DURANGO was originally produced by the Public Theater (Oskar Eustis, Artistic Director; Mara Manus, Executive Director) in association with Long Wharf Theatre (Gordon Edelstein, Artistic Director; Joan Channick, Managing Director) in New York City, opening on November 20, 2006. It was directed by Chay Yew; the set design was by James Ostling; the costume design was by Linda Cho; the lighting design was by Paul Whitaker; the sound design was by Fabian Obispo; the general manager was Seth Shepsle; the production stage manager was Buzz Cohen; the stage manager was Christina Lowe; and the production manager was Ruth E. Sternberg. The cast was as follows:

JERRY/NED .... Ross Bickell
BOO-SENG LEE .... James Saito
JIMMY LEE .... Jon Norman Schneider
THE RED ANGEL/BOB .... Jay Sullivan
ISAAC LEE .... James Yaegashi

CHARACTERS

BOO-SENG LEE — A fifty-six-year-old Korean man.

ISAAC LEE — Boo-Seng's son. Twenty-one, awkward.

JIMMY LEE — Boo-Seng's other son. Thirteen, well-developed for his age.

THE RED ANGEL — A beautiful, blonde, young sun god.

BOB — Boo-Seng's coworker, a white man in his late twenties, early thirties. Played by the actor who plays the Red Angel.

JERRY — A security guard in his late fifties.

NED — A retiree in his fifties or sixties. Played by the actor who plays Jerry.

PLACE

The Southwest.

TIME

The near present.

DURANGO

1

Lights up on Isaac with a guitar. He sings.

ISAAC.
Main Street isn't busy much anymore;
the girl diver's become a lonely sight.
She's a neon girl all dressed up with nowhere to go
and soon she'll be diving in the dark.

Who thought this would be some kind of big destination?
Who stays in all these dusty motels?
The girl dives into a sign that says, "Vacancy."
You see her dive and then you just drive on.

Oh whoh oh
whoh oh
Oh whoh oh
whoh oh

Doesn't she ever, doesn't she ever get lonely?
And doesn't she ever, doesn't she ever get bored?
Doesn't she ever get sick of what she's doing?
I think she wants to hit the road.

Oh whoh oh
whoh oh
Oh whoh oh
whoh oh

Main Street isn't busy much anymore;

the girl diver remains a lonely sight.
She's a neon girl all dressed up with nowhere to go
and she's diving in the dark.

2

An office. Boo-Seng is sitting behind the desk. Jerry, a security guard, sits in a chair. Boo-Seng's desk is clean except for a framed photo.

BOO-SENG. How old are you, Jerry?

JERRY. Letsee now ... fifty ... fifty-eight.

BOO-SENG. You can retire soon.

JERRY. Yeah, if I last that long.

BOO-SENG. Full benefits.

JERRY. That's the idea.

BOO-SENG. And then what?

JERRY. Oh, I don't know ... maybe travel. Play golf. See my grandkids more. Usual stuff, I guess.

BOO-SENG. Back where I come from, you know, lot of my old friends, they are quite successful now.

JERRY. Is that so?

BOO-SENG. One is the owner of his own company, big company. Another is very high in the government, you know, close to president. Another is president of university.

JERRY. Must be quite a reunion when you guys get together.

BOO-SENG. No, I haven't seen them in long time.

JERRY. Why not?

BOO-SENG. I haven't gone back in over twenty years.

JERRY. Not even once?

BOO-SENG. Here is my home.

JERRY. Sure. *(Jerry reaches for the framed photo.)* These your boys?

BOO-SENG. Yes.

JERRY. Good-looking kids.

BOO-SENG. This one, Jimmy, he's a swim champion. No one can beat him in backstroke.

JERRY. He looks like a winner.

BOO-SENG. He is. He'll get scholarship for swimming I'm sure.

Which is good. Hard to get into college without some kind of, you know, special thing.

JERRY. Yeah, grades aren't enough anymore. Getting so competitive.

BOO-SENG. And my other son, Isaac, he's going to be doctor. He just came back from his interview at the University of Hawaii. That's in Honolulu. Very good med school. Very hard to get in.

JERRY. Tell me about it. My Lisa applied everywhere and only got in one place — and that was by the skin of her teeth.

BOO-SENG. Your daughter? Is in med school?

JERRY. Doctor now. One more year of residency. Pediatrics. *(Jerry hands the photo to Boo-Seng, who puts it into a box behind the desk. Boo-Seng sets the box on the desk.)* You ready?

BOO-SENG. Jerry? Sometime, in the morning. I don't know my face. Inside, I still feel the same, same as when I was young …

JERRY. … exactly the same …

BOO-SENG. … but then I have this old face. *(Pause.)*

JERRY. Would you like a moment, Mr. Lee? *(Boo-Seng nods.)*

BOO-SENG. Thanks, Jerry.

JERRY. Don't mention it. *(Pause. They sit there.)*

BOO-SENG. Jerry. Maybe a moment … alone?

JERRY. Well, if it were up to me, of course, but —

BOO-SENG. What am I going to do?

JERRY. Oh, I know you wouldn't *do* anything, it's just … you know the rules.

BOO-SENG. *(Softly:)* I don't want everyone see you walk me out like I'm a criminal.

JERRY. It won't be like that. *(Boo-Seng cleans out his last drawer. There are letters and a brochure. The brochure is old and folded up. He unfolds it and looks at it. Maybe, very briefly and very faintly, there is the sound of a breeze, of wind moving through leaves.)* Mr. Lee? I have to be at another office by four. Let's go. *(Boo-Seng puts the brochure in his pocket. He picks up the box and stands.)*

BOO-SENG. Yes. Let's go.

The kitchen. Isaac is playing the guitar. Jimmy is stirring something in a pot.

JIMMY. I thought Dad told you to get rid of that.

ISAAC. Screw Dad. You gonna tell him I still have it?

JIMMY. Nah, I don't care if you play. So what was it like?

ISAAC. Warm.

JIMMY. Duh, warm. Arizona's warm. I mean, what else?

ISAAC. It's a totally different kinda warm. Arizona's putrid warm. Arizona's like the armpit of the United States warm. And Honolulu ... Honolulu's like the promised land. I mean, they've got soy sauce at the fucking McDonald's, right by the ketchup. You can get kimchi at the corner store, that's what I'm talking about.

JIMMY. No.

ISAAC. Yes! And everyone goes around in swimsuits, I shit you not. Grocery shopping, filling up their gas — in swimsuits, man, girls and guys. And they're all beautiful. Tan. Slender. You've never seen such beautiful people. I didn't see a single pimple on anyone the whole time I was there.

JIMMY. What'd you do after your interview?

ISAAC. I don't know. Just hung out.

JIMMY. Didja talk to any girls?

ISAAC. Yeah ... but no one really interesting. I mean, they *look* good, but. *(He shrugs.)*

JIMMY. I can't wait to visit.

ISAAC. You know how hard it is to get into med school, Jimmy?

JIMMY. It's hard.

ISAAC. Shit yeah, it's hard. And for someone who isn't exactly a four-oh, organic chemistry major who also runs a homeless shelter on the side, one might even say it's impossible.

JIMMY. But you got to the interview, that's a good sign, right? Right?

ISAAC. Check this out. Listen to this chord. *(He plays a chord.)* Isn't that a cool fucking chord? I just found it.

JIMMY. You know, we had an assembly today and the marching band from your old high school came and played. And the sax

player, he played the theme from that old show they show on TV sometimes, *The Benny Hill Show*. It was pretty funny.

ISAAC. Uh-huh. *(He looks at his fingers.)*

JIMMY. It made me think. Made me think of quitting swimming.

ISAAC. *(Not listening:)* Sure. *(Listening:)* What?

JIMMY. I could do something else, right?

ISAAC. Like what?

JIMMY. I could learn to play the sax.

ISAAC. Jesus, why not just pick up the clari-fucking-net?

JIMMY. I kinda want to be in a band.

ISAAC. Oh, you're killing me. You are NOT going to be a band geek, Jimmy, okay? Over my dead body.

JIMMY. I think band would be more fun than swimming. It's like when you swim, you swim alone. But when you're in band ... you're in a *band*.

ISAAC. Do you *want* to get picked on? Is that it?

JIMMY. Look, it's not like when you went to school. I don't let myself get picked on.

ISAAC. You think I *let* myself get picked on?

JIMMY. Joining math club, what did you expect? *(The sound of the front door opening.)*

ISAAC. Shit. *(He hides his guitar and starts setting the table. Boo-Seng enters.)*

JIMMY. Hey, Dad.

ISAAC. What's up. *(Boo-Seng walks right through the room without acknowledging either Jimmy or Isaac. He leaves. Jimmy and Isaac just look at each other.)*

JIMMY. Is he okay?

ISAAC. Is he ever?

JIMMY. *(Calling offstage:)* Dad? Dinner's ready. *(Jimmy puts rice on the plates and then puts beef stew on the rice. Isaac starts eating. Jimmy sits down. Boo-Seng enters and sits at the table.)* How was your day, Dad? *(Boo-Seng closes his eyes, as if deep in thought. He breathes heavily. Jimmy looks at Isaac, who just shrugs. They eat in silence. Boo-Seng finally opens his eyes. He clears his throat.)*

BOO-SENG. Tell me what you think. *(Pause.)*

JIMMY. 'Bout what, Dad?

BOO-SENG. I think it is time for family trip. *(Isaac looks alarmed. Jimmy looks eager.)*

| JIMMY. | ISAAC. |
| Really? | What? |

ISAAC. Dad, I just got back from a trip. I'm tired.

BOO-SENG. What tired? You sit on plane, that's all.

ISAAC. But I've got classes, you've got work —

BOO-SENG. I have some time off ... I always thought you need to see more of where we living.

ISAAC. What's to see? It's all the same, it's all dirt and rocks.

BOO-SENG. Jimmy need to see.

JIMMY. Cool. When can we go, Dad?

BOO-SENG. This weekend.

ISAAC. I have to study. You know, for my bio test on Monday and orgo and —

BOO-SENG. Just a short trip. Drive up north maybe. Take a look around, drive back. Different up there. Not desert. Tree.

ISAAC. Yeah, but Jimmy's probably got a swim meet, right, Jimmy?

JIMMY. No, we don't have a meet until — ow! *(Isaac has kicked Jimmy under the table.)* Coach said we could have the weekend off to — quit it, Isaac.

ISAAC. But you need to rest, *right, Jimmy?*

BOO-SENG. He can rest in car.

JIMMY. Yeah. So where we going, Dad? Where d'you want to go?

BOO-SENG. Durango.

ISAAC. What the hell's that?

BOO-SENG. You don't know Durango? Everyone know Durango. *(He takes out the brochure and looks at it.)* There is train ... Very famous train. Silver train. It leave from Durango and go up into the mountain.

JIMMY. Durango.

ISAAC. Never heard of it.

BOO-SENG. It's famous.

ISAAC. Well, never heard of it.

JIMMY. Is it a long trip?

BOO-SENG. No. Just a few hours.

JIMMY. We could do that, Dad, if you want to.

BOO-SENG. I wanted to for long time. Now is last chance, maybe. *(He puts the brochure away.)*

JIMMY. Yeah. Soon Isaac'll be in Hawaii.

ISAAC. Yeah.

JIMMY. Then let's do it. C'mon, we can do it, right?

ISAAC. I don't feel up for it ... I'll stay here and watch the house, someone's gotta watch the house, right?

JIMMY. You can't just not go. It's a family trip.

ISAAC. Well, I don't want to go, okay? I just got back from one trip, I'm not / about to go on —

JIMMY. But we've never done this, we've never all gone on a trip.

ISAAC. Yeah, we have.

JIMMY. *I* haven't.

BOO-SENG. We leave tomorrow morning.

ISAAC. Does anyone hear a word I'm saying? No.

JIMMY. You're going.

ISAAC. *You* go, go with Dad. Have fun.

JIMMY. *(To Boo-Seng.)* Dad. You gonna just let him punk out on us? *(Boo-Seng sets down his fork and frowns.)* What is it? What's wrong?

BOO-SENG. Somehow ... Doesn't taste right.

JIMMY. Did I make it wrong?

BOO-SENG. No ...

ISAAC. Maybe he's just sick of Dinty Moore Beef Stew. Are you, Dad? Are you sick of Dinty Moore Beef Stew? *(Boo-Seng gets up.)*

BOO-SENG. I'm going lie down. Jimmy. I will wake you at six. *(Boo-Seng leaves.)*

JIMMY. C'mon, Isaac. Please.

ISAAC. Gee ... let me think about it no. *(Isaac scrapes the food off Boo-Seng's plate onto his own plate and starts eating. Jimmy looks at him in disgust. Mouth full:)* What? Did you want some too?

JIMMY. Such a jerk. *(Jimmy leaves.)*

ISAAC. *(Calling:)* You're not exactly a ray of sunshine either. *(Isaac stops eating. He gets his guitar from where he hid it. He holds it but doesn't play.)*

4

Jimmy's room. Jimmy is sitting at his desk, drawing in a sketchbook. Isaac knocks at the door.

ISAAC. C'n I come in?

JIMMY. No. *(Isaac comes in anyway.)* I said no.

ISAAC. What're you drawing? C'n I see?

JIMMY. Go away. *(Isaac flops down on Jimmy's bed.)*

ISAAC. Your bed is so much more comfortable than mine. I don't get that. How come you get the better bed? Oh, wait, I know, it's because: *(Imitating their father:)* An athlete needs his sleep. *(It's a joke they usually share, but Jimmy keeps ignoring him.)* Yeah … I should take up a sport. Hey, Jimmy, can you think of a non-strenuous sport? Jimmy. Hey.

JIMMY. Go to your own room.

ISAAC. Why do you want to go on this road trip, huh? It'll be dead boring. Cooped up in a small car with Dad and me. I mean, Jesus, is that your idea of a good time?

JIMMY. That's not the point. The point is he asked. He asked to spend time with us. He never asks that.

ISAAC. What're you talking about? He goes to every single one of your swim meets.

JIMMY. Yeah, and you know what he does? He comes, sits in the last row of the bleachers and he times me. And then he writes down all the times in this little book and after I swim, he comes and finds me, and tells me down to the last tenth of a second how far off I am from my personal record or the city record or whatever. Sometimes I'll be like getting ready for my next event, like at the starting blocks right before the relay or something, and he'll just come barreling up and I can't make him shut up, he'll just stand there, rattling off all these times at me while I'm putting on my goggles. It's like he's there to check up on me, not to support me. And definitely not to spend time with me. And the one time he offers to spend time with us — all of us together — you act like he's just asked you to chop off a limb.

ISAAC. I get carsick.

JIMMY. Shut up, you love to drive.

ISAAC. Jimmy.

JIMMY. Just get out.

ISAAC. Jimmmmy. You know what I remember? After all those trips? What I remember is how we drove hours and hours to get to the Grand Canyon. And it wasn't even where we were headed. We were just going up to Flagstaff but Dad had to go see the Grand Canyon — no, he had to pretend he was going to see it really *for us,* for me and Mom. 'Course me and Mom just want to go home; we're hungry, we're tired, but does Dad care? No. So we drive and we drive and we finally get there. But it's taken us so long that now it's sunset. Five minutes after we park, the sun's gone down and I can't even see my hand in front of my face let alone the Grand

fucking Canyon. I mean, shit. The Painted Desert. The Petrified Forest. Yellowstone. Yosemite. Bryce Canyon. Zion Canyon. Monument Valley. I am so fucking *sick* of national monuments. All those hours and hours on the road with Dad screaming his head off about how "we are going to have a good time OR ELSE" and Mom not saying a word — *a word*. I get sick just thinking about it.

JIMMY. But that was a long time ago.

ISAAC. So? You think this shit changes? It doesn't change.

JIMMY. It's not fair. It's not fair that you got to go see all these places and then by the time I get big enough no one wants to go anywhere anymore.

ISAAC. Why do you think it's going to be so great?

JIMMY. I'm not expecting it to be great. I just want to go. It doesn't have to be this great adventure. But you, me and Dad, we never do anything all together. Let's just go, Isaac. Please. Let's just go. *(Pause. Jimmy turns back to his drawing.)* You *are* selfish.

ISAAC. Who says? Dad? Or you?

JIMMY. Me. *(Beat.)*

ISAAC. All right … You want to go so bad … show me what you're drawing.

JIMMY. What? No. Why?

ISAAC. 'Cause I'm curious. You're always drawing. See your light on late at night. All secretive.

JIMMY. Forget it.

ISAAC. Hey, I thought you wanted to go …

JIMMY. Even if I did show you, you'd just welsh on the deal.

ISAAC. Welsh? What kind of word is welsh?

JIMMY. You going to renege on this deal?

ISAAC. Ooh, renege. What is that, an SAT word? Fine. I won't *renege*. I promise. *(Jimmy gives Isaac the sketchbook.)*

JIMMY. Just this page. Don't flip around. *(Isaac looks at the sketchbook.)*

ISAAC. Superheroes? You're drawing superheroes?

JIMMY. It's my comic, shut up.

ISAAC. Nah, it's good. Really.

JIMMY. Yeah, right. Just give it back. *(Jimmy grabs it from him.)* That's enough.

ISAAC. Didn't know you could draw like that.

JIMMY. Deal's a deal, right? *Right?*

ISAAC. Yeah. What the hell. I'll go.

JIMMY. You'll see — it'll be fun.

ISAAC. Uh-huh.

JIMMY. It'll be like, like, the three of us together. And maybe Dad will finally be, you know. Happy. With us.

ISAAC. Night, Jimmy. Get some rest. You're going to need it. *(Isaac salutes and leaves.)*

JIMMY. What's that supposed to mean? *(Calling:)* What's that supposed to mean? *(He turns back to his desk. He starts drawing again. The Red Angel appears. He is a beautiful, blonde, young man.)* He grew up in a small, dusty town. He was just an average kid. *Or so he thought.*

RED ANGEL. Did I know I was different? Somehow, somewhere? Was there, underneath it all, some kind of recognition?

JIMMY. The morning of his thirteenth birthday, two little bumps appeared beneath his shoulder blades.

RED ANGEL. They terrified me. I hid them with sweaters, I never took off my backpack. But no matter what I did, they grew larger and larger.

JIMMY. And then: tragedy! His house was on fire! He made it out but his parents were trapped! They waved frantically from the second-floor window — who could save them?

RED ANGEL. And then I understood —

JIMMY. — who he was —

RED ANGEL. — what I was —

JIMMY. — the bumps on his shoulders:

RED ANGEL. They were wings. *(The Red Angel unfurls his wings. Jimmy lifts up his drawing into the air, as he makes a sound of flying.)*

5

The family car. Isaac slouches in the front seat. Boo-Seng sits behind the wheel, alert. Jimmy's bouncing around the back.

BOO-SENG. Air conditioner off?

JIMMY. Check.

BOO-SENG. Back door locked?

JIMMY. Yup.

BOO-SENG. Side door?

ISAAC. Why do we have to leave so early?

BOO-SENG. Have to get early start. I don't like to drive when it's too hot. Uh ... *(He's lost his place.)* ... back door ... Jimmy, what was I — ?

JIMMY. Side door. And check.

BOO-SENG. Window locked?

ISAAC. ... Oh, for Christ's sake ...

BOO-SENG. *(Sharp:)* Isaac, this is important.

JIMMY. Windows are locked. Check.

BOO-SENG. Okay. Okay. Let's go. *(He starts the engine. The car gets underway. Boo-Seng smiles. He's glad to be on the road.)*

JIMMY. *(Sing-songy.)* Road trip, road trip. We're going on the road —

ISAAC. Shut up, Jimmy.

BOO-SENG. So quiet outside.

ISAAC. That's because it's six friggin' A.M. in the morning.

BOO-SENG. Clear weather. Good sign. What is word for that? Good sign?

JIMMY. Lucky?

BOO-SENG. No ... *Aus*-pi-shss.

JIMMY. *(Correcting him:)* Aus*pi*cious.

BOO-SENG. Aus-*pi-shuss.*

JIMMY. Auspicious.

ISAAC. Someone wake me up when we're there. *(Isaac settles in and closes his eyes.)*

BOO-SENG. Isaac. You know. I wanted to say. That was very big job you did. Go to Hawaii and come back by yourself.

ISAAC. It's no big deal.

BOO-SENG. So what did my friend say when you saw him?

ISAAC. What friend?

BOO-SENG. My friend, I told you, I gave you his number.

ISAAC. Oh, I didn't see him.

BOO-SENG. What?

ISAAC. I got busy. Plane was a little late ... and then I had to get ready for the interview ...

BOO-SENG. But I told him you would call him. I told him. Isaac. This is serious.

ISAAC. Well, I'm sorry.

BOO-SENG. He is a busy man, Isaac. He did you great favor.

ISAAC. I know. You don't have to remind me, okay?

BOO-SENG. He is my oldest friend; he was *waiting* for you.

19

ISAAC. Well, you didn't tell me that.

BOO-SENG. He was *expecting* you.

ISAAC. Then why did you make it sound like I should *maybe* just call him up? That's what you said: *Maybe* you can call him *if* you have time.

BOO-SENG. That means call him.

ISAAC. Then why didn't you say so? Say: *You Have To Call Him.* Don't make it sound like it's an option if it's not.

BOO-SENG. Are you so stupid, you can't understand what I mean?

ISAAC. It's not my fault you don't just say what you mean, I'm not some friggin' / mind-reader.

BOO-SENG. The most basic thing, and you can't even / do what is right.

ISAAC. Look, I filled out fifteen med school applications for you. I got on an airplane for ten hours for you. So don't tell me I don't / do anything for —

BOO-SENG. For me? FOR ME? Is THAT what you think it's for?

ISAAC. Of course it is, so that you can tell your friends that your son is a doctor so that you'll look good, right?

BOO-SENG. I DON'T CARE ABOUT LOOK GOOD. You don't have any talent to be anything else, *that's* the point. Selfish *ba-boh. Ee na-pu-nom seh-ki.* My friend, you know how long we know each other? Since we are twelve years old. I remember how poor we were. We were always hungry. And in the winter, our hands were cold —

ISAAC. *(Muttering, underneath:)* Yeah, yeah, yeah …

BOO-SENG. — no gloves —

ISAAC. Just one holey mitten that you had to, like, share among all seven of your brothers and sisters …

BOO-SENG. You have no idea what is like to be cold. To be hungry. A hundred degree below freezing —

ISAAC. That's impossible.

BOO-SENG. YES IS POSSIBLE. A hundred degree below, up in the mountains. That's why Americans had such hard time, because not used to how cold it get and hungry, you never know how hungry —

ISAAC.	BOO-SENG.
(Talking under his father:) Once a month, if we were lucky, we got a little bit of bone with a little flap of marrow hanging from it	There was never enough to eat. If my friend or I got some money, we would buy

and my brother, he was the favorite, a little food and then we so he always got the bone to gnaw would eat it — on together, share —

BOO-SENG. *(He cuts Isaac off wherever he is.)* **He is my best friend.** He did so much for you and you, / you —

ISAAC. FINE, DAD, I'm a horrible person, okay? Your friend was kind enough to pull strings to get your loser of a son an interview and how do I repay him? By not calling him up and falling over myself thanking him. I'm useless, I'm an idiot. I'm hopelessly spoiled. You're absolutely right. I should've never been born — you and Mom should've ABORTED ME WHEN YOU HAD THE CHANCE. *(A silent fury fills the car. Jimmy sits quietly in the backseat. A long silence.)*

JIMMY. *(Tentatively.)* So. When will we get there? Dad? Dad, when d'you think we'll get there? I'll look in the map. Where exactly is Durango? Near Flagstaff or …

BOO-SENG. Colorado. *(An enormous pause fills the car.)*

ISAAC. What?

BOO-SENG. What.

ISAAC. What did you say?

BOO-SENG. I said Colorado.

ISAAC. Durango's in Colorado?

BOO-SENG. *(An affirmative grunt.)* So?

ISAAC. You said a few hours. That's what *you said.* I asked, how far and you said —

BOO-SENG. The train is a few hours. Just up and down the mountain. Once you get there.

ISAAC. Are you KIDDING me?

BOO-SENG. DON'T SHOUT.

ISAAC. Are you telling us this stupid train is in COLORADO?

BOO-SENG. SO?

ISAAC. YOU DIDN'T TELL US THAT.

BOO-SENG. I SAID DON'T YELL. **Durango is in Colorado, everyone know that.**

ISAAC. WE didn't. We didn't know that we were embarking on a trip that actually crossed STATE LINES.

BOO-SENG. LINE. State LINE. Arizona, Colorado. THASSIT.

JIMMY. It's not so bad, Isaac, just don't —

ISAAC. SHUT UP, JIMMY. Stop the car.

JIMMY. We're already on the way —

ISAAC. I'll hitch a ride home —

BOO-SENG. Let him go, fine! Feel sorry for whoever pick him up!
JIMMY. NO. Dad, don't pull over. C'mon, Isaac. This is supposed to be a family trip.
ISAAC. Family? Family??? I've been kidnapped.
BOO-SENG. WHO KIDNAP? **I am your father.**
JIMMY. Just calm down, everyone, okay? Dad? Isaac? It's fine. We'll go, we'll see the train or whatever, we'll come back. No big deal. Okay? Okay.
ISAAC. Colorado. Colorado! *(A long silence.)*
JIMMY. I always wanted to go to Colorado.
ISAAC. Shut it, Jimmy. Just. Shut it.

6

Jimmy and Isaac look out the window of the car. They are unbelievably bored.

BOO-SENG. Now, if we compare with United States, Korea is very small country. But Korea has very long history. Unfortunately, only a little bit of the history is written down. Only two thousand year out of maybe five thousand. But there are many thing to be proud of. Pottery. Korean pottery: very good. And Kum Kang Sam, which is very beautiful mountain, in fact the most beautiful mountain in the world. But unfortunately, it is in North Korea, so we cannot go see it. There are many trees in —
JIMMY. Right there, Dad — pull in.
BOO-SENG. Uh?
ISAAC. There. *There.* Don't miss it, you're missing it —
BOO-SENG. I see it, I see it. *(Boo-Seng turns in. He stops the car.)* Okay. *(Boo-Seng stops the car and Isaac and Jimmy jump out of the car like animals that have been let out. Calling after them:)* That is the first Korea lesson. We continue after lunch. *(Boo-Seng sits in the car.)* Aus-pi-*shus*. Aus-pi-shus. *(Lights up on Bob.)*
BOB. Hey, Boo. You got a minute? Step into my office. Let's have a talk. *(Bob's office. They sit down.)* You know I like you, Boo. Always have. You've been a good team member.
BOO-SENG. My reports are always good, right, Bob?

BOB. They're very accurate, it's true. That's why I try to watch out for you. Because I know that among the team, there's the tendency to, sometimes, to exclude you —

BOO-SENG. Somehow people are not comfortable around me. I don't know why.

BOB. Now, I wouldn't say that. But I wanted to speak with you about your progress reports.

BOO-SENG. My reports are good, you said that.

BOB. No, I'm not talking about the reports you make. I'm talking about the reports on you. Job performance, Boo. Some members of the team are … how can I put it … concerned about you.

BOO-SENG. Concerned? Why?

BOB. Yes. It seems … well, there are some areas where you're a bit … less effective … team building … communication skills …

BOO-SENG. Maybe I get too focus on my project, on my work, but that's not a problem.

BOB. Well, Boo, it kinda is. When you don't attend team exercises, staff meetings —

BOO-SENG. Two meetings, I didn't go because no one *told* me —

BOB. There are memos, Boo, it's not anyone's job to — look. You've been a good worker, that's not the issue. But you know we lost that big contract, and they're looking to dissolve two of the ten units at this location and one of them, one of them, is yours. Now, we're trying to relocate people, but it's just not possible in every situation, I mean, in every case. We simply don't have that many openings, Boo. I'm sorry.

BOO-SENG. I'm sorry?

BOB. It's not my decision, I mean, if I had my way —

BOO-SENG. You are telling me what? Say it clearly.

BOB. I am saying it clearly, Boo. Clear as I can. I'm sorry, I'll slow down. It's not just you we have to lay off, fifteen percent / of the workforce —

BOO-SENG. But but but I have this watch, you gave me this watch, see? There was a cake. Twenty years of service. See?

BOB. That's right and that's for you to keep and I'd be happy to be a reference / for you to anyone —

BOO-SENG. To who? Who's going to hire me, Bob? I'm fifty-six.

BOB. I know, I know —

BOO-SENG. In four years, I can retire with full benefits, Bob — Bob.

BOB. You'll get a good severance package, Melissa in HR will /

take care of —

BOO-SENG. Who's going to pay my health insurance?

BOB. Severance comes with five months' paid insurance, after which I'm sure / there are some great values.

BOO-SENG. You gave me this watch. You want it? Take it. Take it. *(He starts to take it off.)*

BOB. No, no, Boo, it's yours. C'mon. I don't want it. You've earned it. Just think of it as early retirement. Travel. Huh? When was the last time you went somewhere? Or take up golf. There's a golf course on every block. Just keep it in perspective, okay? It's not the end of the world. Now, I've got a meeting …

BOO-SENG. **Don't walk away from me, Bob.**

BOB. What, you threatening me, Boo?

BOO-SENG. No, no, of course I'm not —

BOB. 'Cause I'll call security, I will.

BOO-SENG. I'm fifty-six, Bob.

BOB. My hands are tied, Boo. My hands are tied. *(The office is gone. Boo-Seng looks at his watch. He takes it off and then he hurls it from him as far as he can. On his naked wrist is the pale outline of where the watch used to be.)*

7

On the patio of a fast food place. Isaac and Jimmy sit at a table, eating.

JIMMY. He'll be bigger than Batman, bigger than Spiderman. The superhero of the future.

ISAAC. Hate to break it to you, but Stan Lee? Not Asian.

JIMMY. I *know* that.

ISAAC. I'm just saying …

JIMMY. Look, it's not an issue. My superhero's going to be normal. He's not going to be, you know, like us.

ISAAC. Well, excuse me.

JIMMY. I just don't want to be limited.

ISAAC. Look in a mirror, Jimmy. What do you think you are? All right. What're his powers?

JIMMY. I haven't figured it all out yet. But he's basically invulnerable.

ISAAC. So nothing can hurt him?

JIMMY. He's sort of like Superman except without kryptonite.

ISAAC. Well, that won't work.

JIMMY. What do you mean?

ISAAC. Superheroes are *defined* by their flaws.

JIMMY. I don't want my superhero to have any flaws. That's the point. He always wins.

ISAAC. That's boring.

JIMMY. Is not. Shut up.

ISAAC. Think about it: Charles Xavier — stuck in a wheelchair; Nightcrawler — looks like a freak. It's like that. You have to have some kind of irony because that's how life is. It might be supercool you can read minds or whatever, but it's got to come at some great cost.

JIMMY. But why? Why does it have to cost you something? Why can't you just have the cool powers?

ISAAC. Because then it's not real.

JIMMY. So?

ISAAC. Okay, who's your favorite?

JIMMY. Who do you think? Wolverine.

ISAAC. And why do you like Wolverine?

JIMMY. 'Cause he kicks ass.

ISAAC. Wrong. You know what makes Wolverine so compelling? All the other X-Men, their powers tend to be big and dramatic. But Wolverine's power is simple: He's got a healing factor, that's it. Everyone else, their powers *prevent* them from getting hurt. But with Wolverine, it's the opposite. Wolverine was *made* to get hurt. He was *made* to suffer. That's what his gift *is*. And because he suffers, because he feels pain, we see in him the truest expression of what we, as humans, experience. *That's* why he's the greatest X-Man. Not because he's the most powerful but because he's the most human. So this comic, the Red Angel? He's all powerful, fine. But what makes him human? What is it about him that when we look at him we see ourselves? *(Pause.)*

JIMMY. Wow. I didn't know you liked Wolverine so much.

ISAAC. I don't. I like Magneto.

JIMMY. What? He's like pure evil.

ISAAC. Yeah, but you know what makes him human? Two words: the Holocaust. He's the best fuckin' villain ever, and you know why?

Because you sense that maybe, just maybe, he coulda been a hero. Maybe, if the world hadn't fucked him over so much, he mighta been someone — done something — good. *(He throws his crumpled-up food wrappers at the trash basket. He misses.)* He still over there? *(Jimmy looks past Isaac at Boo-Seng, who is doing old-fashioned stretching exercises, e.g., rotating from side to side, rotating his arms, etc.)*
JIMMY. Yeah.
ISAAC. What's he doing?
JIMMY. I have no idea. *(Isaac turns around and looks.)*
ISAAC. Oh God. Come on. *(They get up. Jimmy looks at his palm.)*
JIMMY. I wish I were a mutant. *(Isaac looks at their father.)*
ISAAC. I think we kinda already are. *(They walk towards Boo-Seng.)* Dad. Dad! What're you doing?
BOO-SENG. Stretching. Good for back.
ISAAC. Someone's going to see you.
JIMMY. Are you hungry, Dad? We brought you some food —
BOO-SENG. No. Not hungry. *(Isaac and Jimmy get in the car.)*
JIMMY. C'mon, Dad. Let's get a move on. *(Isaac leans on the horn.)*
ISAAC. Let's go! *(Lights go briefly up on Jerry.)*
JERRY. Mr. Lee? Let's go.
BOO-SENG. Yes. Let's go. *(Boo-Seng gets into the car. They drive away. Boo-Seng waves goodbye to Jerry, who waves back. Jimmy looks back.)*
JIMMY. Who you waving to Dad?
BOO-SENG. Jerry. *(Jimmy and Isaac look back but don't see anyone. They look at each other and Isaac just shrugs. They drive on.)*

8

Time has passed. The car. Jimmy sits in the front. Isaac is in the back.

BOO-SENG. So after the king invented his own alphabet, then we had *hang-gul.* Very smart man. But still, you know, we use Chinese character for some thing. For instance, in the —
JIMMY. Dad — where's your watch?
BOO-SENG. What?
JIMMY. Your watch.

BOO-SENG. I lost it.

JIMMY. What? Where?

BOO-SENG. It fell off.

JIMMY. You loved that watch.

BOO-SENG. No.

JIMMY. You hardly never took it off.

BOO-SENG. I only like because it was free.

JIMMY. Listen, Dad, maybe you should eat something? We brought you some food.

BOO-SENG. I feel fine.

JIMMY. You're probably hungry.

BOO-SENG. No ... I feel good. Clean.

JIMMY. Well, how about just some fries for now. Isaac, hand me the fries.

ISAAC. Oh ... were you saving those?

JIMMY. Isaac! Those were for Dad!

ISAAC. Well, no one said — *(The car hits something with a loud thud as Boo-Seng swerves.)*

JIMMY. Dad!

ISAAC. What the hell was that? *(Boo-Seng pulls over to the side of the road.)*

JIMMY. Something ran out, I saw it. *(All three get out of the car. They look down at the bloody body of an animal.)*

ISAAC. Oh, God ...

JIMMY. It's a dog.

ISAAC. No shit, Sherlock.

JIMMY. Where'd it come from?

ISAAC. I don't know.

JIMMY. It's gotta belong to someone.

ISAAC. It's still breathing. *(Boo-Seng goes to the trunk of the car and walks back to the front holding a hammer.)*

JIMMY. It's in pain, Isaac. Isaac, do something. Isaac!

ISAAC. What do you want me to do?

JIMMY. I don't know, help it.

ISAAC. Do I look like a friggin' vet?

JIMMY. We can't just let it suffer.

ISAAC. I *know* that, will you just — *(Boo-Seng quickly swings the hammer down onto the dog's head. It lands with a sickening sound. Isaac and Jimmy both jump.)* Jesus. *(Silence. Boo-Seng throws the bloody hammer away. He gets into the car.)*

BOO-SENG. Let's go. *(Jimmy and Isaac get in the car. Jimmy in*

front, Isaac in back. No one says a word.)

9

Night. The Palms Motel. A room with two double beds. Isaac is fiddling with the AC. Jimmy comes in from the bathroom.

JIMMY. I just stunk up the bathroom, royally.
ISAAC. Thank you for sharing.
JIMMY. Why's it so hot?
ISAAC. AC's on. Be patient. *(Jimmy gets into a bed.)* What do you think you're doing?
JIMMY. Going to bed.
ISAAC. So share with Dad. That bed's mine.
JIMMY. That's not fair.
ISAAC. All right, but touch me while I sleep and you're a dead man. *(Jimmy settles in.)*
JIMMY. He still out there? *(Isaac looks out the window.)*
ISAAC. Yeah.
JIMMY. What's he doing?
ISAAC. I don't know. He's just standing by the pool. Like staring at the water.
JIMMY. He hasn't said anything for the last few hours.
ISAAC. Gee, how unlike him.
JIMMY. But it's not like usual. It's not like he's angry, he's just … I don't know.
ISAAC. Ugh. Fucking motel smell. I feel like I'm six years old again.
JIMMY. I kinda like it. Smells clean.
ISAAC. Trust me, it ain't that clean. I don't get it. Shouldn't we be there by now?
JIMMY. Well … maybe we were kind of going the wrong way for a little bit.
ISAAC. What?
JIMMY. I was looking at the map in the car and I don't think Dad knew where exactly he was going. He took this long route that kind of dead-ended. I think he tried it thinking it was a shortcut, but it doesn't connect back up to the interstate. It looks like it does but I think that's just the crease of the map.

ISAAC. So he was doubling back?

JIMMY. … Yeah.

ISAAC. Oh God. Why didn't you say anything?

JIMMY. I didn't know. Not till it was too late. And you were asleep so … Anyway, we're almost there. I bet we'll get there by noon.

ISAAC. No, we won't. We'll be in the desert forever. Like Moses. We'll fucking die here. *(Isaac doesn't move. He's splayed out on the bed, like he's been shot.)*

JIMMY. Well, I'm going to sleep. *(He turns off the light.)* Good night, Isaac. Good night, Isaac. Good night —

ISAAC. Good night. *(Outside, Boo-Seng stands by the pool. It emits a green glow. The water and light cast shapes and patterns on Boo-Seng's face. He kneels down. He washes his hands, rubbing them hard. There's blood on his shirt from the dog. He tries to wash that too. Tears seem to seep from his eyes. He washes his face and the water from the pool mingles with his tears. He stares into the water. He is exhausted and spent. Ned enters.)*

NED. There something in there?

BOO-SENG. Wha? *(Boo-Seng stands.)*

NED. In the pool?

BOO-SENG. Oh. No. Just the light in the water …

NED. Kind of hypnotizing, isn't it? You staying here?

BOO-SENG. Yes. With my boys.

NED. I'm here with the wife. Grand Canyon. You?

BOO-SENG. Durango.

NED. Durango!

BOO-SENG. You know it?

NED. Of course I do! Durango! It's famous!

BOO-SENG. It is!

NED. Everyone knows Durango!

BOO-SENG. Exactly! So you been to Durango?

NED. No. Would like to. You know, someday.

BOO-SENG. Are you retired?

NED. Yup. Look it, don't I? It's the hat. Kids gave it to me. I hate it.

BOO-SENG. How do you like it? Retirement?

NED. Oh, it's great. Plenty of time. Freedom. Get to travel, do whatever I want. *(Pause.)* I'm bored out of my fucking mind.

BOO-SENG. I am too. I am bored out of my fucking mind.

NED. Since you retired?

BOO-SENG. Since … always.

NED. *(With perfect understanding:)* Yeah … Yeah. May I offer you

a beer?

BOO-SENG. *(He is about to say no.)* Yes.

NED. Wait right here. *(Ned leaves. He returns with a beer. He and Boo-Seng sit on lounge chairs.)* Ned Harmon.

BOO-SENG. Boo-Seng Lee.

NED. What is that?

BOO-SENG. Korean. *(Ned leans in.)*

NED. *Ahn-nyung-ha-seh-yo. (Boo-Seng looks at him confused.)* Means hello! *(Boo-Seng smiles and nods.)*

BOO-SENG. Yes. Hello.

NED. Don't you speak your own language? *(He laughs.)* So. Boo-Seng. How long you been retired?

BOO-SENG. Oh, I'm not ... I was laid off.

NED. Holy shit. After how many years of service?

BOO-SENG. Twenty.

NED. Twenty! Those bastards! I was a teacher — high school — so thank God I didn't have to deal with that kind of shit. Used to be that a company would take care of its own. But not anymore. Everything's disposable now. People most of all. So bottoms up, my friend. Bottoms up. *(They drink.)*

BOO-SENG. Being teacher is very important job.

NED. I like to think so. I mean, yeah, it could be a pain in the ass, but at the end of the day, you got to watch these kids grow and change. And sometimes kids would come back, kids I'd taught years before who now had kids of their own. And that always felt good. To be remembered. How about you? Did you like what you did?

BOO-SENG. ... Funny, you know? You look back at your life ... at all the things you chose ... and ... you don't know how you got here.

NED. So true.

BOO-SENG. I did not like my work. But I did it. Every little thing have to be put into computer. Make a report and another report and another. All day long, every day, day after day ... I did. And if I didn't get laid off, I would still be there, doing. And I would feel ... lucky. Lucky to have someplace to go every day. But why? Why did I want so little? Where did I learn to want so little for myself?

NED. Well ... what is it you want now?

BOO-SENG. I ... I want ...

NED. Go on ... just say it. What? *(The enormity of all the things Boo-Seng wants silences him.)*

BOO-SENG. I don't know. Not anymore. Too late. All of it. Too

late. *(He is utterly lost.)*

NED. Hey … it's okay … *(Ned puts his hand on Boo-Seng's leg. Boo-Seng jumps to his feet, almost knocking the beer out of Ned's hand.)* Whoa, whoa —

BOO-SENG. I'm sorry, I — I — it's late —

NED. No, no, no, I shouldn't've —

BOO-SENG. I am very tired, too much time in car —

NED. No prob, my wife's probably wondering where I am anyway. It was nice talking to you. Have fun in Durango. And good luck to you.

BOO-SENG. Thank you. For beer.

NED. Don't mention it. Well. Take it easy. Hey, how do you say, "Take it easy"?

BOO-SENG. I don't think there is expression for that. *(Ned leaves. The motel room.)*

JIMMY. *(Whispering.)* Isaac? *(Louder.)* Isaac? *(Louder.)* Isaac! Are you awake?

ISAAC. I am *now.*

JIMMY. I can't sleep. C'n I ask you something?

ISAAC. C'n I stop you?

JIMMY. What was it like? To be part of a family?

ISAAC. You are part of a family.

JIMMY. But a whole one.

ISAAC. Shit, I don't know. Why're you thinking about this now?

JIMMY. I think about it a lot. Don't you? *(Pause. Isaac does.)* She was a good cook, right?

ISAAC. Yeah.

JIMMY. What was her best dish?

ISAAC. Wasn't like that. Everything she made tasted good. She could pull food out of the fridge like a magician pulls a rabbit out of a hat, make stuff out of nothing. And she always smelled good, like really good. Not like perfume. Just the way she was. The smell of her skin.

JIMMY. Do you think she'd like me? How I've turned out?

ISAAC. Yeah, Jimmy. I think she'd like you a lot. I was the one who was too much trouble.

JIMMY. You were?

ISAAC. Oh yeah.

JIMMY. Why?

ISAAC. I dunno. I always pushed her, tried to see how far I could get. She was always having to wale on me. Keep me in line. Don't

know why I'm that way but I am. Not like you.

JIMMY. What do you mean?

ISAAC. You're a good kid, that's all. You try to make people happy. Try to make things easier.

JIMMY. I don't mean to.

ISAAC. No, it's a good thing. People *like* you; you get along. That's important.

JIMMY. You wanna see something? *(Jimmy goes over to his sketchbook. He slides out a plastic sheath — a cut-down version of the kind that usually holds comics. Inside the plastic is a photo and a white piece of poster board. Jimmy carefully takes the photo out and shows it to Isaac.)*

ISAAC. Where'd you get this?

JIMMY. It was in a photo album in Dad's closet. I found it when I was looking for Dad's old trench coat for my Halloween costume last year. You remember? How I went as a detective?

ISAAC. Yeah.

JIMMY. It was up on a shelf. This one's from Christmas. It's you and Dad and Mom and me. She looks happy, huh?

ISAAC. You keep it with you?

JIMMY. Yeah. Was it a good Christmas?

ISAAC. No. I don't think it was.

JIMMY. Why not?

ISAAC. They fought. They fought a lot. *(Isaac hands the photo back to Jimmy. Jimmy carefully takes it from Isaac and slips it back into the bag. And then he carefully slips it back into his sketchbook.)* Doin' much sketching on this trip?

JIMMY. Nah. You know why I draw?

ISAAC. 'Cause you're bored?

JIMMY. No. It's like, like lotta times ... lotta times I *need* it. I need to draw. I think it started when I was really little. I was copying some panel of Cyclops, you know, after Jean Grey dies. And she's going to come back, you know, be reborn as Phoenix, except he doesn't know that yet. And I'm drawing him and then I see these, like, dark spots on the paper? And I can't figure out what they are. And then I realize they're tears. I'm drawing his face, but it's *my* face ... I mean, it's the same. My face is all ... like in the same expression as the picture. Isn't that weird? That I feel what I draw? That it's the only time that I really feel anything?

ISAAC. Did you think ... Mom was Phoenix?

JIMMY. I'm not a moron, Isaac. People aren't superheroes. People

are just people. And they don't come back. *(A moment.)*

ISAAC. Hey, you want to hear about this movie I saw once?

JIMMY. What movie?

ISAAC. It's called *Motel Hell.*

JIMMY. Shut up, Isaac —

ISAAC. These people are staying at this motel that's got, like, a diner attached? And this diner is known for its amazing steaks, like the most tender, juicy steaks in the world. And this is all based on a true story.

JIMMY. Stop it.

ISAAC. Listen, it's not scary. Thing is, people start *disappearing* from the motel. And it turns out —

JIMMY. Shut the hell up, I mean it / la la la la la la la I can't hear you la la la la la —

ISAAC. It turns out that the cook — the cook is like killing them in their sleep and then dismembering the bodies and putting them in the freezer and — *(The sound of a splash outside.)* What the hell was that? *(Isaac springs out of the bed.)*

JIMMY. What? What's going on? *(Isaac opens the door.)*

ISAAC. Jimmy, stay here.

JIMMY. Where're you going? Isaac! *(Isaac rushes out. Jimmy sits up, a little freaked out. He opens his sketchbook.)* The Red Angel haunts the city at night. He hides in the shadows and no one ever sees him pass by. *(The Red Angel appears.)*

RED ANGEL. He wears a mask so no one can see his face.

JIMMY. His eyes are cruel. The Red Angel is compassionate towards two things and two things only: children …

RED ANGEL. And animals.

JIMMY. In his spare time, he plays the sax. *(Suddenly, a yellow water polo ball bounces across the stage. Jimmy and the Red Angel look after it.)*

RED ANGEL. Aren't you going to get that? *(Neither moves. The door opens. The Red Angel disappears. Isaac reenters with his arms slung around his father, helping him in. Boo-Seng is soaked.)*

JIMMY. Dad! Are you okay?

ISAAC. Get some towels. *(Jimmy runs to the bathroom and reenters with an armload of towels.)* Here, take off your clothes. We'll hang 'em up to dry.

BOO-SENG. Turn off the light.

ISAAC. You're getting all modest now?

BOO-SENG. I'm your father. Turn off the light. *(Isaac turns off*

the light. Boo-Seng takes off his shirt and pants. Isaac throws his clothes over the chair and Jimmy helps towel Boo-Seng dry.)

JIMMY. What happened?

BOO-SENG. I … lost my balance.

ISAAC. You could've drowned, Dad. Give me your clothes. You done? Come on. Get in bed.

BOO-SENG. Cold …

ISAAC. Just get under the blanket. *(Boo-Seng gets in bed. Jimmy gets in his.)*

JIMMY. *(Whispering:)* He okay?

ISAAC. Yeah.

JIMMY. He didn't eat today.

ISAAC. He didn't? *(Boo-Seng shifts in the bed. They continue to talk in lowered tones.)*

JIMMY. No — the food we got him is still in the bag in the car. Isaac. He is okay, right?

ISAAC. Yeah, Jimmy. Just — go to sleep. *(Isaac pulls Jimmy's blanket up and tucks him in. Suddenly, the neon sign of the motel switches on. It consists of three parts, aligned vertically. The top section is a girl piking in mid-air. The middle section is the girl straight in the air, diving towards the water. The bottom section is the girl entering the water with a splash. A soft glow beats on the room as each part of the sign lights up in succession. The girl dives again and again. Isaac sits there with that rhythm of light on him. One-two-three. One-two-three. One-two-three.)*

10

Isaac remembers his mother.

ISAAC. *(As his mother.)* Isaac-ya, why you still awake? *(She sighs.)* I know. Sometime sleep not come. My father was like that. I am like that. Maybe you are like that too, mm?

    He was banker, you know. Very smart, kind of genius. He could look at whole row of number — big number — and add all up in his head, no paper, no pen, nothing. We were so wealthy we had a telephone, very first one in whole town. Our phone number was six. But it was little useless you know, because there was no one to call.

I was plainest of five girls. When I was born, my father was quite discourage. So when you were born, I sent him photo and you know, he write me back right away saying: *This one going to be big man, important man.*

I was so proud to have son. Should not matter, but everyone like first one to be boy. And second one, boy or girl is okay. So this baby *(She touches her stomach.)* boy I am happy, girl I am happy. Okay, maybe little happier if girl, but that's secret, okay?

Isaac-ya. You want another secret?

(She whispers:) You are always my first baby. My very first one. And you are most special, because you are first baby I ever, ever love. And no matter how much I love new baby, I never, ever love in exact same way I love you. Okay? Okay. Happy? Happy. Good. Now go to sleep. Give me kiss. *(She is kissed.)* Such good son. When you want to be. But I know my father was right. Big man. Great man. Everything is inside you. It just take time.

11

Morning. The motel room. Boo-Seng is gone. Isaac heaves the blinds up so that the sun pours in, waking Jimmy.

JIMMY. Turn it off. *(He turns over and pulls the blanket over his head.)*
ISAAC. Rise and shine.
JIMMY. Where's Dad?
ISAAC. Waiting for us. Get up. *(He snatches all the blankets off Jimmy's bed.)*
JIMMY. Isaac.
ISAAC. Up! Here. *(He tosses him a toothbrush.)*
JIMMY. Where'd you find a toothbrush?
ISAAC. Front desk. Toothpaste is on the sink. *(Jimmy stumbles out of bed and into the bathroom.)* Gotta get a move on. I want to be there by lunch. Sooner we get there, sooner we get home. *(Jimmy opens the door. He's brushing his teeth.)*
JIMMY. You were talking in your sleep.
ISAAC. I was?
JIMMY. You said — here, I wrote it down. *(He opens his notebook.)*

I think it says — it was dark — "The sun is mittens. Hold the dime."
ISAAC. What does that mean?
JIMMY. You said it. *(Jimmy goes back into the bathroom. The door opens and Boo-Seng enters with two cups of coffee.)*
BOO-SENG. Ready?
ISAAC. Yeah, almost. *(Boo-Seng hands a cup to Isaac.)* Thanks. You sleep okay? *(Boo-Seng nods. Boo-Seng seems a little embarrassed about the previous night and Isaac doesn't pursue it. Instead, they drink their coffee. Jimmy comes out of the bathroom.)*
JIMMY. Where'd you get that?
BOO-SENG. Lobby. It's free. *(Boo-Seng and Isaac are clearly savoring the coffee.)*
JIMMY. Can I have some?
ISAAC. Since when do you like coffee?
JIMMY. What, I can't drink coffee?
BOO-SENG. I'll go check out.
JIMMY. I'll come with. *(Boo-Seng and Jimmy leave. Isaac sees Jimmy's sketchbook. He hesitates and then opens it. He finds the photo and looks at it. A page catches his eye. He stares at it hard. He flips around and stares at some other pages. He puts the photo in the sketchbook back and sets it back where he found it. Jimmy appears at the door.)* Hey.
ISAAC. Hey. No coffee?
JIMMY. They were out. What're you doing?
ISAAC. Nothing. *(Jimmy grabs his notebook and goes to the door.)*
JIMMY. You coming? Dad's waiting for us in the car.
ISAAC. Yeah. Let's go.

12

The car. Isaac is driving. Jimmy is in the passenger side, reading the map. Boo-Seng is asleep in the backseat.

ISAAC. Lots of interesting stuff in this area, you know that, Jimmy? Ruins, that big ol' hole in the ground where that comet hit … all sorts of stuff. Ghost towns too. You want to stop and see some of it?
JIMMY. I thought you were sick of tourist sights.

ISAAC. Yeah, but some of it ... like Four Corners, you know, standing in four states at once. It's kind of cool.

JIMMY. I just want to get there.

ISAAC. Sure, no prob. *(Isaac looks back to make sure Boo-Seng is still asleep. Boo-Seng is quietly snoring away. Isaac pulls over to a rest area.)*

JIMMY. What are you doing?

ISAAC. Let's get out of the car. Stretch our legs a little.

JIMMY. Dad, you want to —

ISAAC. Just let him sleep. He looks like he needs it. *(They get out of the car and walk several yards away.)* So Jimmy: Can I ask you something?

JIMMY. Okay ...

ISAAC. How's school?

JIMMY. That's your question?

ISAAC. One of 'em.

JIMMY. It's fine.

ISAAC. Kids make fun of you?

JIMMY. No.

ISAAC. How about girls, any cute girls?

JIMMY. Isaac, why we are we talking about this?

ISAAC. Well, it's like ... I thought we should have a talk. Man to man. You know, Dad never taught me how to shave. It's a simple thing, right? The kind of thing a man should teach his son. But he never showed me. So for years, I shaved the wrong way. I shaved against the grain. Which you're not supposed to do. I mean, I guess some guys do it because it's a closer shave or whatever, but most guys, you get ingrown hairs and cuts if you shave against. You're supposed to shave *with*. But see, I didn't know this. So I'm talking years of bad shaves. Bleeding. Pimples. And when I finally figured it out, I was so mad because he could have just told me, you know? So see, Jimmy, there are things, like, man things that men pass on to each other. And you're getting to be about that age when you and I should talk about, talk about ... well, I should tell you about ...

JIMMY. You want to show me how to shave?

ISAAC. Sex, Jimmy. Maybe we should talk about sex.

JIMMY. Yeah, like you know anything about sex.

ISAAC. I know more than you. Anyway, this isn't about me. I wanted to ask you, Jimmy, and you can be honest, okay? Are you ... *(He lowers his voice and says something very, very quietly in Jimmy's ear.)*

JIMMY. What??? NO.

ISAAC. C'mon, Jimmy, it's me, you can tell —

JIMMY. Why would you even ask that? Why would you even *think* that? *You're* the one who's never even had a real girlfriend, I mean, what's *that* about —

ISAAC. Yeah, well *I* don't draw figures of naked men, do I?

JIMMY. What?

ISAAC. Jimmy, I'm sorry, I wanted to look at that photo of Mom again and your sketchbook was sitting there and I didn't —

JIMMY. YOU JERK.

ISAAC. The fact is, I saw them, Jimmy. I saw them.

JIMMY. Those were figure studies, asshole.

ISAAC. Well, I didn't see any figure studies of female superheroes. And last I checked, superheroes actually wore costumes, they didn't go around naked. With enormous erections. *(Silence.)* So are you?

JIMMY. No.

ISAAC. 'Cause you know, I —

JIMMY. I'm not. I'm not a … I like girls. I want a girlfriend. Heather Spiro, she's got a crush on me. Her friends all say so.

ISAAC. Well, I'm sure she's very cute.

JIMMY. There're a coupla guys like that in my class and you can tell, everyone can tell. Way they talk. Way they walk. I'm not like that.

ISAAC. Well … good. 'Cause you know, it's not that I've got anything personal against gays, I mean, I like Erasure, you know —

JIMMY. Don't be such a hypocrite, you totally hate fags and you know it.

ISAAC. That's not true —

JIMMY. Anything you don't like it, you say it's "gay" —

ISAAC. It's an expression.

JIMMY. Don't lie.

ISAAC. Jimmy, I don't have anything against homosexuals, okay? But our family is built on a very simple equation. And that equation is that you are the golden boy — the savior — and I am the fuck-up. Do you realize, I mean, I don't even know if there is a Korean word for "homosexual." I don't know if Dad has even the slightest idea what that is. So I'm just saying, it's a good thing you're not … [gay]. If you were, I'd still love you, we'd still be brothers, all that stuff. But life — our life, yours, mine and Dad's — would be a hell of a lot harder. Because that man's got his hopes built on you. You're his golden boy, his favorite —

JIMMY. Oh, come on.

ISAAC. You are! You are. You know you are.

JIMMY. But that's not fair — I never asked for that. How come I have to be the hope of the family? You're the one who's going to be a doctor, who's going to med school —

ISAAC. Yeah, well … I'm not sure about that …

JIMMY. Are you kidding? Dad's oldest friend practically runs the program —

ISAAC. Well, you're the swim champion who's going to get a full ride anywhere you want to go.

JIMMY. No, I'm not.

ISAAC. You've got coaches drooling all over you —

JIMMY. I quit the team.

ISAAC. What?

JIMMY. I quit the team.

ISAAC. You quit the team?

JIMMY. Yes, because I hate it. I've always hated it.

ISAAC. What are you talking about? You love the water. You're like a fucking fish. You win every meet you go to.

JIMMY. Doesn't mean I like it.

ISAAC. You can be that good at something and not like it?

JIMMY. Yeah. In fact, you can hate it.

ISAAC. *(Pause.)* Well. I didn't go to my interview.

JIMMY. What?

ISAAC. I didn't go.

JIMMY. Bullshit. Dad took you to the airport, picked you up.

ISAAC. No, I went to Hawaii. I just didn't go to the interview.

JIMMY. Isaac.

ISAAC. I made it to Honolulu. Got to the hotel … I even steamed my suit, you know, ran the shower and let my suit hang. Like they say to do. And I walked out of the lobby with every intention of getting into a cab and going to the University of Hawaii. I gave myself plenty of time to spare. But I never made it. You know what I did instead? I went to some outdoor mall. There was like this little café and I sat at this tiny plastic table with an umbrella over it. I felt like I was in a tropical drink. There was some kind of bad open mic going on. I sat there until the sun went down. And then I went back to the hotel room and watched porn till dawn. Dad's going to kill me. *(Beat.)* The porn cost a lot. *(Jimmy looks at him, speechless. Finally:)*

JIMMY. Well. Was it any good?

ISAAC. No. As a matter of fact, it sucked.

JIMMY. What was it?

ISAAC. I think it was, um, *Edward Penishands. (Jimmy starts to smile.)* You think this is funny? *(Jimmy starts laughing.)* Well, I'm glad you think this is so funny. Dad's going to kill me and you think it's funny. *(Isaac starts to smile too. They both start to laugh, really laugh, the contagious kind that escalates the more they try to stop. The laughter finally subsides. They are quiet.)*
JIMMY. Maybe it's good. I mean, you don't have to be a doctor. You could do other stuff.
ISAAC. Yeah, 'cause there's so much stuff I'm good at.
JIMMY. You could be a musician.
ISAAC. I don't want to be a musician, Jimmy.
JIMMY. Why not?
ISAAC. Because it's something I just do for me. And besides I suck at it, the way I suck at most things.
JIMMY. That's not true —
ISAAC. I'm not like you, I'm not good at everything I touch, which, I mean, do you have any idea how *annoying* that is?
JIMMY. You just don't try —
ISAAC. What are you talking about? You think you were the only one to try swimming? You think they didn't throw me into a pool and hope that I'd be the next Mark fucking Spitz? What a joke that was. I was hopeless in the water. But one day, you just kinda stumbled into the water when no one was looking and that was that. I mean, no one even had to teach you how to swim, you just *knew.* Sometimes I think the only thing that kept me from smothering you in the crib was how fucking cute you were, all innocent and shit, like you were brand shiny new and maybe I could help keep you that way. I mean, you're even good at things you hate. Who does that?
JIMMY. I don't hate swimming. I mean, I don't *like* it, but. That's not why I quit.
ISAAC. That's not why you quit.
JIMMY. No. I quit because. It's stupid.
ISAAC. If it made you quit, it's not stupid.
JIMMY. No, it didn't, I mean, nothing *made* me quit. *(Beat.)* Sometimes we end practice early. Coach lets us go.
ISAAC. Uh-huh.
JIMMY. So I was waiting for Dad to come pick me up. And me and Charlie, we're throwing around one of the water polo balls. 'Cause we're so bored. But Charlie, he's such a dumbnut, he throws the ball too far. It goes way above my head, right into the shed. Shed's where they keep everything, you know, lanes, the big clock that times us,

40

the kickboards, everything. So I go in there to get the ball and it's real dark, right? There's no light in the shed, so I can barely see where I'm going and I hear this sound, and I think it's me knocking into something except then I realize I haven't really moved, that this sound isn't me, that I mean, I didn't make it. Someone else is in there. And it's this guy. This senior. He's in there changing. He's by this small, high window, I guess 'cause it's the only place where he can see what he's doing. But thing is, he's standing in the only place where I can see him too. And I guess it's no big deal, I mean, I see other guys all the time in the, you know, the locker room or whatever. But this guy ... he is. Different. *(The Red Angel appears. We see him as Jimmy must have seen him: golden in the light, sculpted, like a David come to life.)*
ISAAC. Different how? *(Jimmy can barely breathe.)*
JIMMY. Different ... perfect. He's perfect. *(The Red Angel picks up the ball.)*
RED ANGEL. Here. You looking for this? Hey. Kid? You okay? Take the ball. Take it.
JIMMY. I couldn't move.
ISAAC. Why?
JIMMY. I don't know.
RED ANGEL. What's wrong with you? Take the ball.
JIMMY. I turned and ran.
ISAAC. Why? Did he do something?
JIMMY. No. But he called me a, a —
RED ANGEL. Hey — you —

JIMMY.	RED ANGEL.
— little faggot.	— little faggot.

RED ANGEL. **Take the goddamn ball.** *(He hurls the ball at Jimmy. He is gone.)*
ISAAC. Why'd he call you that?
JIMMY. Because he saw my, he saw my. I couldn't help it and he saw my. So I ran.
ISAAC. You got a?
JIMMY. Yeah. That happens, right? I mean just 'cause one guy makes me — that's happened to you, right? *(Isaac tries to nod his head "yes" but it turns into a shake "no." He doesn't know what to say.)*
      I don't want to be a faggot, Isaac.
      I don't think I'm a faggot.
      I'm *not* a faggot.
      I am not. (A beat.)
ISAAC. Then. I guess you're not. *(Silence. Jimmy holds out his pinkie.)*

41

JIMMY. Don't tell Dad. Please. *(Isaac squeezes Jimmy's pinkie with his own.)*
ISAAC. Tell him what.

13

Jimmy imagines his mother.

JIMMY. *(As his mother.)* Dear Jimmy,
  You have to understand that sometime not all my words are good. English is hard language, you know?
  I am dying. Maybe in Korean I could come up with more better, more beautiful way to say, but in any language, it is same sad. But maybe it is good you never see me old or sick. Not have to clean my poo or wash me. I am like Marilyn Monroe, always young and pretty.
  You know in Korean I am very funny. I always used to make everyone — even your father — laugh. But somehow in American I have lost all my humor.
  But to matter at hands. I have a few thing to tell you. Help Isaac and Dad. They are both exact same: stubborn. You are third way. Very gentle, like my mother. So you can help them. You have big heart, Jimmy. I can tell. So you can love them and love *for* them when sometime they cannot.
  Other thing: Be good. Dad has lot of pain. Story too long for here. But he has lot of sadness. Kind of disappoint. Having good children maybe help heal him. I was not such good wife, maybe. That is another long story. Be kind to your father. He may seem hard but inside he is more easy to break than you think.
  Last thing: This is my recipe for my special *kal-bi*. Some day, you marry nice girl and you can make this together, eat and be happy.
  Because most of all, be happy. This is the thing I wish for you.
  Love, Mom.

14

The car. Isaac is driving. Jimmy is in the backseat and Boo-Seng is in the passenger side. They're both asleep. Isaac sings quietly.

ISAAC.
>*I don't have the greatest voice*
>*I don't have the sharpest mind*
>*All I have is a few worn tools*
>*and a lot of my own time*

(Isaac hears music.)

>*I don't have the brightest face*
>*I wasn't born with the cleverest hands*
>*All I have is a few good chords*
>*and the lack of any plan*
>
>*Making a lot with just a little*
>*Making what you can with what you got*
>*Days pass and the hours run out*
>*whether you made something or not*

(The music begins to taper off or maybe it's already gone.)

>*So if you don't mind, I would rather be singing*
>*Even if my voice slips off the key*
>*I know I was not made to sing*
>*but I hope singing will make me.*

Boo-Seng wakes up.

BOO-SENG. Where are we?

ISAAC. Hey. Sleep okay?

BOO-SENG. Where are we?

ISAAC. Colorado somewhere. We'll be in Durango soon. *(Boo-Seng rubs his eyes.)*

BOO-SENG. Thank you. For driving.

ISAAC. No problem. *(Pause.)*

BOO-SENG. Isaac … I know you didn't want to come. But you'll like Durango. I know you will. It is very beautiful place.

ISAAC. Sure. *(Pause.)*

BOO-SENG. When we get home, I want you to call my friend.

ISAAC. What friend? The one in Hawaii? Why?

BOO-SENG. To apologize. *(Slight pause.)*

ISAAC. Fine.

BOO-SENG. You know, he never had kids. I always send him picture of you and Jimmy, he kind of watch you grow up. And he was so looking forward to —

ISAAC. Yeah, I get it, I'll call him. *(Pause.)* So how come he never had kids?

BOO-SENG. Never marry. Surgeon is very busy you know.

ISAAC. Well, if you guys were such good friends, how come we never met him?

BOO-SENG. Mom and him not get along so well.

ISAAC. Why?

BOO-SENG. She didn't like we spend so much time together. But he was my oldest friend. He was … like Gregory Peck, you know? That's what he look like. Very smart. Very strong. No one could make him do anything.

ISAAC. *(Carefully:)* Did someone make you do something?

BOO-SENG. No, but. You know, my marriage to your mother was arranged. We meet and then we decide to marry. Just one time. Very different, huh? Okay, you are okay, we marry. That's how it was. My friend … he didn't understand. He said I was being cow-

ard. But I said to him: You want to choose what you want to be, but that is not for our generation. You and me — we are just laying foundation. That's all. Just laying foundation.

ISAAC. Sure.

BOO-SENG. Isaac? Maybe when we get home, I could buy you another guitar.

ISAAC. I thought you said it was a waste of time.

BOO-SENG. It is, but road is almost done. You did interview. Once you get in, then that is big job finished. So you deserve something you want. A reward. A new guitar. A better one. But not too expensive.

ISAAC. That's, uh ... Thanks. *(Pause.)* Hey, Dad? You know, Jimmy and I were talking. And ... it sounds like he's under a lot of stress, you know. School. Swimming. Anyway, I thought maybe, maybe he should stop doing so much.

BOO-SENG. Busy is good.

ISAAC. Yeah, but the swimming takes up a lot of time, don't you think?

BOO-SENG. Jimmy love to swim.

ISAAC. But that's the thing, Dad, I don't think he does —

BOO-SENG. What do you know? You never love anything in your life. Jimmy love to work hard. Like me. That's why he is honor student. All-city —

ISAAC and BOO-SENG. — champion in one-hundred-meter backstroke —

BOO-SENG. — *and* two-hundred-meter IM —

ISAAC. All I'm saying is, what's the big deal if he takes some time off swimming?

BOO-SENG. How's he going to go to college if he doesn't swim?

ISAAC. Jimmy's smart, he'll get some money like I did —

BOO-SENG. I mean a *good* college, not state.

ISAAC. Look, I just want him to be happy, don't you want him to be happy?

BOO-SENG. Jimmy is happy.

ISAAC. How do you know? Have you asked him?

BOO-SENG. **I don't have to ask.**

ISAAC. Right, 'cause you know us *so* well.

BOO-SENG. I don't have to ask Jimmy because Jimmy is very honest, clear.

ISAAC. And I'm not?

BOO-SENG. No. Always act one way, then another —

ISAAC. Like when?

BOO-SENG. Many time.

ISAAC. Name one.

BOO-SENG. Family Day.

ISAAC. What?

BOO-SENG. Family Day.

ISAAC. And again: What?

BOO-SENG. **Bring Your Family to Work Day.**

ISAAC. Okay, that was like five years ago.

BOO-SENG. *I* remember. I remember I bring my son, my son who I am SO proud of to work. Straight-A student. Rank number two in class — could've been number one but you didn't work hard enough. I introduce you to my co-workers and then I turn around and what do I hear? They're saying, *Hey, Isaac, how you understand your father? His English is so bad!* And you laugh and say, *I know. But lucky for me, I am fluent in bad Asian accents.*

ISAAC. I didn't — it was the first thing that popped into my head —

BOO-SENG. You laugh at me so my co-workers will like you?

ISAAC. I was sixteen, I was an asshole, what did I know?

BOO-SENG. No respect, always the same, you never think before you talk, just like your —

ISAAC. *At least she talked.* She wasn't a **FREAK** who holds things in for like *five, fucking / years.*

BOO-SENG. **Put on brake. I said, PUT ON BRAKE.** *(Isaac pulls over. Boo-Seng gets out of the car and slams the door shut. He walks away from the car, trying to cool himself off and calm down. Jimmy has been awake and listening.)*

JIMMY. Isaac? What just happened?

ISAAC. I don't know, we just talking and then —

JIMMY. What did you do?

ISAAC. What did *I* do?

JIMMY. Dad? *(He starts to get out of the car and go towards Boo-Seng.)*

BOO-SENG. Jimmy, **stay in the car.** *(Jimmy retreats. He hits Isaac on the shoulder.)*

JIMMY. What is wrong with you? Why do you do this?

ISAAC. Do what?

JIMMY. You make him like, implode. Why can't you just leave him alone?

ISAAC. I was trying to help *you,* you little asshole.

JIMMY. Who says I need your help? All you ever do is make

things worse.

ISAAC. Man, who the fuck made it Pick on Isaac Day?

JIMMY. Dad. Dad. C'mon. Get in the car. Please. (*Boo-Seng walks over to the driver's side. He opens the car door and Isaac flinches. He motions to Isaac to get out.*)

ISAAC. What? (*Boo-Seng gestures even more furiously. Isaac hits the steering wheel hard and then gets out. Boo-Seng sits in the driver's seat. Isaac walks away from the car. He takes a moment and then opens the back door of the car. To Jimmy:*) Get out. Take the front. I said, TAKE. THE FRONT. (*Jimmy gets out and gets into the passenger side as Boo-Seng starts the car. He burns rubber and they're off.*)

16

Boo Seng remembers his wife. She's a little drunk. She is speaking in Korean but we understand her in English. There is no trace of an accent.

BOO SENG. (*As his wife.*) Please stop yelling, you're giving me a headache. And it's your fault anyway: You should've hidden your beer better. It tastes awful, by the way, I don't know how you can drink it. God, I hate how cheap you are.

You should hide your letters better too. (*She holds up the brochure. It is new.*) It looks very pretty. I'm sure you'll have a wonderful time. Of course, it's not as beautiful as Hawaii, but it's a lot closer isn't it? Who knew you had such a burning desire to see … Colorado. (*She throws the brochure down.*) I don't want to fight. I am too tired. So I am not going to tell you not to go. If you want to go see him, go. You're a free man. You have a choice.

But, husband. I do have some news. I saw my doctor. (*She puts her hand on her left breast.*)

It is bad.

And it has spread.

So tell me.

What would you like to do?

17

A small park in Durango, Colorado. It's a beautiful, clear day. The light is sun-dappled. Jimmy and Boo-Seng sit on a bench.

JIMMY. God, I am *so* glad to be out of that car. So is this it? Is this what you wanted to see? *(Boo-Seng looks around.)* What are you doing?
BOO-SENG. Trying to imagine. What it was like. In the past. *(They sit in silence.)*
JIMMY. *(Looking off:)* Wish he'd hurry up. How much you think the tickets are, huh, Dad?
BOO-SENG. Jimmy?
JIMMY. … Yeah?
BOO-SENG. Do you like swimming?
JIMMY. … Sure.
BOO-SENG. You don't do it because I … make you do it?
JIMMY. No, Dad. Why're you asking?
BOO-SENG. Well. Isaac said.
JIMMY. What. What'd he say?
BOO-SENG. That you don't like swimming so much.
JIMMY. Let's talk about it later, okay, Dad? When we get home.
BOO-SENG. Because you know, it's important. It will help you for college. I can't … I can't anymore.
JIMMY. What're you talking about, Dad?
BOO-SENG. I thought … I thought my accuracy will protect me. That I do a good job, no one else can do such a good job. But accuracy is not enough. Twenty years and then gone.
JIMMY. What do you mean, gone?
BOO-SENG. I mean gone. Like my watch. *(He bares his naked wrist.)* What I've done. What I am. All gone. *(Isaac enters. He looks a little stunned. He slowly sinks onto the bench.)*
ISAAC. There're … no more tickets. The last train left three hours ago. They only run two a day. And we missed the second. We missed it. *(He starts to laugh helplessly.)* But get this? They were sold out anyway! Turns out you have to make a reservation months in advance. Reservations, can you believe it? This stupid train is so popular that apparently you have to make reservations! Who knew?

Girl at the ticket office looked at me like I was an idiot when I asked for tickets for the next train. She's like, "What do you think this is? Grand Central?"

BOO-SENG. No train?

ISAAC. That's right, Dad. No train.

BOO-SENG. Tomorrow?

ISAAC. No. They're sold out till next month.

BOO-SENG. I didn't know …

ISAAC. Obviously.

BOO-SENG. I didn't know.

ISAAC. What kind of person doesn't *plan* this kind of thing, doesn't at least LOOK UP the —

JIMMY. Isaac, lay off —

ISAAC. NO. I can't believe I fell for it AGAIN. But you were like, oh, please, Isaac, a family trip, it'll be fun — *(To Boo-Seng:)* **What a fucking waste of time.**

JIMMY. Stop yelling at him!

ISAAC. I mean, what kind of moron, what kind of / loser —

JIMMY. I mean it, Isaac. LAY OFF. *(He pushes Isaac away from Boo-Seng and Isaac pushes Jimmy back, hard.)*

ISAAC. God, the way you kiss his ass.

JIMMY. You're the one who's a loser, Isaac.

ISAAC. You're such a fucking daddy's boy, Jimmy.

JIMMY. You're the one can't even show up for your own stupid —

ISAAC. SHUT UP. *(Pause.)* All right. You want to go there? Okay, fine. Let's go. Let's fucking go. Dad: I didn't go to my interview.

JIMMY. Isaac.

ISAAC. No, Jimmy, it's okay. It's been eating away at me ever since I got back, so let's just throw it out there. I did not go to my interview.

BOO-SENG. *(To Jimmy:)* What is he talking about?

JIMMY. He did go, he did, he just —

ISAAC. No, Jimmy. I didn't. I didn't go.

BOO-SENG. What?

ISAAC. I'm saying I lied, Dad. About all of it.

BOO-SENG. You didn't go…?

ISAAC. Why does everyone make such a big — I'm never going to get in, doesn't anyone see that but me?

BOO-SENG. But it was ARRANGED. All you had to do was show up — *(He stops himself.)*

ISAAC. Wait, wait — what did you just say? You mean the interview, right? You arranged just the interview, *right? (A long pause.)* Nice, Dad.

BOO-SENG. What.

ISAAC. Way to teach your boy some ethics.

BOO-SENG. What ethics?! You think other people don't have help? Some guy his father donate new science building, you think that is more fair? The one time I can help you, I do it, I help you. What's wrong with that?

ISAAC. Help me? Is that what you think —

BOO-SENG. Everything I do is to help you. But you never appreciate, never once. Ever since you were small, so selfish. Jimmy: *He* is my son.

ISAAC. Right. Your champion.

BOO-SENG. He is a winner. What do you do?

ISAAC. Nothing, Dad. I watch porn in hotel rooms, okay? **That's what I do.** A winner. Hear that, Jimmy? You're a winner. Maybe Dad doesn't understand what he's dealing with here. Shall we enlighten him?

JIMMY. Isaac.

ISAAC. Oh, come on. Let's all be truthful. Honest. Why, not, I've been honest. So come on, Jimmy, don't you have something to share?

JIMMY. ISAAC.

ISAAC. Maybe Dad would wanna see some sketches — oh, excuse me, "figure studies."

JIMMY. Dad, just ignore him —

ISAAC. What, you only like the truth when it comes to *me?*

JIMMY. Shut up.

ISAAC. Doesn't it get cramped in there? In that dark, lonely closet?

JIMMY. I said, SHUT UP. *(Jimmy hits Isaac as hard as he can. Isaac buckles and goes down. He is clearly in pain.)*

BOO-SENG. What are you doing? STOP IT.

ISAAC. Fuck. That hurt. *(Jimmy stands over him, fists clenched. He is bigger and stronger than Isaac has ever realized.)*

JIMMY. I'm not so little anymore, Isaac. And I'm only going to get bigger. So you better be careful. You better watch your fucking back. *(Isaac slowly, painfully stands up.)*

ISAAC. Stupid me. I thought we were going to be honest. *(Pause.)* All right. You win. I'll shut up. *(They sit on the bench. Silence.)* So now what?

JIMMY. We're going home.

ISAAC. After all that …
JIMMY. Well, we're not going to wait around for a month, are we? I'm tired. *(He gets up.)* Come on. Let's go. You heard me. Let's go.
BOO-SENG. Yes. Let's go.

18

The Red Angel appears.

JIMMY. Every now and then, the Red Angel still dreams about it.
RED ANGEL. If I close my eyes, I can see it: the burning house.
JIMMY. One second the window seemed high above him and then suddenly —
RED ANGEL. I'm gripping the frame, twenty feet off the ground.
JIMMY. He looked in the room and saw his parents, huddled in a corner. He picked up his father with one hand and with his other, he grasped his mother around her waist.
RED ANGEL. They were as light as children. When did they become so light?
JIMMY. As the house crumbled around them, he stepped onto the windowsill.
RED ANGEL. I put one foot out into the darkness —
JIMMY. — and jumped. *(The Red Angel is in flight.)* His wings beat in the darkness around them.
RED ANGEL. My family. My father. My mother. Me.
JIMMY. Below, all the neighbors were gathered around —
RED ANGEL. — all of the people I'd grown up with my whole life.
JIMMY. And when the Red Angel finally touched down, shaky from his first flight.
RED ANGEL. I looked around this crowd of people —
JIMMY. — their faces glowing red from the fire —
RED ANGEL. — and I saw nothing but fear on their faces.
JIMMY. They crowded in on him as the house burned and they raised their fists and picked up whatever their hands could find — *(The Red Angel cries out. Silence.)* It turned out that the place where the wings met his back was more delicate than he had realized. *(The Red Angel's wings are gone.)* After he healed, he left the town.

RED ANGEL. You wouldn't even look twice at me now.
JIMMY. He's just a guy with some scars on his back.
RED ANGEL. And when I need to go someplace,

JIMMY.	RED ANGEL.
He just puts one foot	I just put one foot
out into the darkness	out into the darkness

RED ANGEL. and walk. *(The Red Angel walks away. The car. Jimmy is in the passenger side. Isaac is driving. Boo-Seng is asleep in the back. Jimmy opens his window.)*
ISAAC. What're you doing? — I've got the AC on. *(Jimmy takes his notebook out. He opens it and then begins ripping sheets out of it. He tears the sheets up and throws them out the window.)* Stop it. Jimmy. Don't. *(Jimmy keeps tearing up the paper and throwing it out the window.)* Jimmy, not the — *(Out goes the plastic bag with the photo inside. Out goes more paper until the whole notebook's gone and Jimmy's hands are empty. He rolls the window back up. Silence.)*

19

Home. The lights are off. The door opens and Isaac, Jimmy and then Boo-Seng come through the door. Isaac turns on a light. All three sit, exhausted. Wordless. They sit for a long time.

ISAAC. I'm going to bed. *(He stands up.)* I'll call the school tomorrow, okay, Dad? See if I can reschedule. I'll uh. Tell them I had food poisoning. Bad sushi or whatever. Okay? G'night. *(He leaves. Jimmy and Boo-Seng sit together. A long silence.)*
BOO-SENG. He never says sorry. He never just says sorry. *(Silence.)*
JIMMY. Maybe I'll be a doctor.
BOO-SENG. Is that what you want?
JIMMY. Sure. *(Silence.)*
BOO-SENG. *(To himself:)* I want … to do something good before I die. *(Silence.)*
JIMMY. Dad? I love you. *(Jimmy leaves. Boo-Seng goes to the answering machine. There's a message on it. He listens to it. It's the voice of an older man, speaking in Korean. It is Boo-Seng's old friend in Hawaii. Boo-Seng looks at the brochure of Durango. In his room,*

Jimmy sits at his desk but does not draw. In his room, Isaac holds the guitar. He plays a few chords. It's the beginning of a song — the same one we heard at the beginning of the play.)

End of Play

PROPERTY LIST

Guitar
Framed photo
Box of stuff
Letters and brochures
Dinner plates, silverware, etc.
Beef stew and rice
Sketchbook with photo in plastic bag, pencil
Fast food, wrappers, bags
Hammer
Beers
Yellow water polo ball
Towels
Neon diver sign
Toothbrush
2 cups of coffee
New brochure
Answering machine

SOUND EFFECTS

Front door opening
Flying
Car engine
Thud
Message of older man speaking Korean

NOTES
(Use this space to make notes for your production)

DURANGO
Copyright © 2007, Julia Cho

All Rights Reserved

SPECIAL NOTE

SPECIAL NOTE ON SONGS AND RECORDINGS

DURANGO

BY JULIA CHO

DRAMATISTS
PLAY SERVICE
INC.